THE LIFE AND CHARACTER OF THE LATE REV. ISAAC M. COOK,

Pastor of the Presbyterian Church of Bridgewater, Penn'a.

A SERMON,

BY

JAMES ALLISON,

Pastor of the Presbyterian Church of Sewickley, Pennsylvania.

PITTSBURGH:

PRINTED BY W. S. HAVEN, CORNER MARKET AND SECOND STREETS.

1854.

THE

LIFE AND CHARACTER

OF THE LATE

REV. ISAAC M. COOK,

Pastor of the Presbyterian Church of Bridgewater, Penn'a.

A SERMON,

BY

JAMES ALLISON,

Pastor of the Presbyterian Church of Sewickley, Pennsylvania.

PITTSBURGH:
PRINTED BY W. S. HAVEN, CORNER MARKET AND SECOND STREETS.
1854.

SERMON.

"He was a good man, and full of the Holy Ghost and of faith: and much people was added unto the Lord." Acts 2: 24.

The Scriptures are remarkable for their depth and fullness of meaning. A single phrase often expresses a most important truth, which the combined wisdom of the world never discovered, and which the utmost stretch of human thought cannot now fully comprehend in all its bearings. Frequently a solitary expression announces the great fact on which the eternal destiny of men depends; lights up the pathway of human life with an unwonted radiance; gives a glimpse of the glory to be revealed, and fills the soul with thoughts that wander through eternity. It is not unusual for one passage, in a few words, to give a history, concerning which merely human authors would have written volumes. But this peculiarity is most clearly seen in descriptions of character, in which, for sententious brevity, correctness of delineation, and poetic beauty, the sacred writings are altogether unrivalled. We have a striking instance in the Scripture on which we propose to base our discourse to-day. It is spoken of Barnabas, of whom honorable mention is made in several other places in the Acts of the Apostles. He was a Levite by descent, born of parents who dwelt in Cyprus: and he at length became the principal associate of the Apostle Paul in his travels and labors to propagate the gospel. After the death of Stephen, a violent persecution arose against the Church at Jerusalem, by which its members were dispersed abroad throughout the regions of Judea and Samaria, except the Apostles: "and they that were scattered abroad went every where preaching the Word." Some went even as far as Phenicia, Cyprus and Cyrene; "and the hand of the Lord was with them; and a great number believed, and turned unto the Lord." Persecution then, as often since, became the means of spreading the gospel where it had not been previously known, and the blood of the martyrs became the seed of the Church. When the report of these things "came unto the ears of the church which was in Jerusalem," Barnabas was sent to learn the extent of the work, and also to ascertain its true character—"Who when he came, and had seen the grace of God, was glad, and exhorted them all, that with purpose of heart they would cleave unto the Lord." He was not deterred from acknowledging the good that had been done in these Grecian converts, by any Jewish prejudices that might still be found lurking in his bosom; but he rejoiced at seeing the happy effects of the grace of God, and exhorted them, by the highest motives and strongest arguments, to a continued exercise of faith, and a bold profession of the name of Christ, together with obedience to the gospel, whatever they might be called to suffer on these accounts. Then, his character is inimitably drawn by the pen of inspiration. "He was a good man, and full of the Holy Ghost and of faith: and much people was added unto the Lord." "He was a good man"—remarkable for natural affection and kindness: indeed, this is indicated by his name, for it signifies "a son of consolation." He was "full of the Holy Ghost and of faith"—that is, richly endowed with spiritual gifts for the work of the ministry, and possessed of a vigorous faith in the power of the gospel, and of great boldness in time of danger and persecution. "And much people was added unto the Lord"—that is, through his labors, large accessions were made to the Church at Antioch, which became strong and vigorous, afterwards sending forth many teachers to evangelize the nations.

But such gifts and such results have not ceased; and it is our duty to notice and admire them wherever found, *to the praise of the glory of God's grace*, especially when those who possessed such qualities, and accomplished such works, have been removed beyond the reach of our praise or censure. To call to remembrance the virtues of the departed, whom we once knew and still love, is a dictate of nature. This is seen in the care we take of their bodies, the regard we manifest for their relics, the monuments we rear, and the eulogies we pronounce. True, indeed, we will have a more correct image of those to whom we were fondly attached, before our minds, than can be drawn by the most skillful pencil; and in the profoundest depths of our heart will be found a more faithful and imperishable record of their excellencies than can be written by the most truthful pen: but those who were able to influence men for good when alive, will also benefit the living when dead.

Much of the Holy Bible consists of biography—not only of the most distinguished, but also of the most humble. We read of the glory of Solomon, and of the benevolence of the woman who cast two mites—all her living—into the treasury. We read of the wondrous gifts, the amazing self-denials, and the great success of the great Apostle to the Gentiles; and also of the woman who anointed her Saviour's feet, and wiped them with her hair. We have the life of Jesus, and are also introduced to the home of Martha and Mary. The lives of those distinguished in science, art, or literature, are written, and monuments erected to their memory. Those noted for bravery in the army or navy, or for high qualities in the State, are portrayed on the public records and the historian's page; they stand in sculptured marble or molten bronze, or are embalmed in immortal verse. And shall not the Church recount the services and emulate the virtues of those servants of the Lord who have been sent to fight his battles and achieve his victories, "to preach good tidings to the meek, to bind up the broken-hearted, to proclaim liberty to the captive, and the opening of the prison to them that are bound." She has not been slow to honor the memory of those who have occupied high places and been called to an unusual work. The praises of Luther, Calvin, Wesley, Whitefield, Edwards, Chalmers, Alexander and Miller are in all the churches. But in gifts and position they were so far removed from the ordinary course of men's lives, that they can have but little effect by way of leading to imitation upon the people at large. It is more profitable for them to contemplate those who stood more nearly on a level with themselves, and with whom they can feel some kindred sympathy, and who are not so far removed from them as to destroy all reasonable hope of imitation. Most biographies treat of those so widely different in education, pursuits, and traits of character from most men, as to be of little practical benefit to the popular mind: and most works on religious experience are so highly colored as to be positively injurious to many sincere Christians, who never attain to such exalted raptures. We greatly need biographies of common men and women, attractively written, and works on the religious experience commonly enjoyed, prepared in a tasteful and scriptural method. It is therefore becoming in us to-day to view for our improvement the life and character of one of our own aids, whom we well knew, and to whom the words of our text may with great propriety be applied. "For he was a good man, and full of the Holy Ghost and of faith: and much people was added unto the Lord." He was with us, but he is not, for the Lord has taken him. He has laid aside the "mortal" and "put on immortality." He has ceased ministering in the outer court, and entered the inner and upper sanctuary. He has now entered upon the enjoyment of those blood-bought delights on which he loved to meditate, and which he so vividly described. Because of his early removal, the materials from which to form a proper estimate of his life and character, within reach, are comparatively few, but they are sufficient to prove that what was said of Barnabas may also be said of him. He was so eager for heaven that he made but little account of earth; he was so anxious to place jewels in his Redeemer's crown, that he had but little desire to cultivate flowers to be strewed upon his grave when his work would be done. He knew that earthly memorials would fade and crumble, and therefore secured an imperishable record on high. His life properly consisted of two parts—*his youth, and his public ministry.* Children partake greatly of the physical, intellectual, and moral features of their parents: and their whole course of life is greatly dependent on parental pursuits and expectations. Every child is a sacred gift from God to be trained for him. And when the responsibility is duly felt and the training faithful and scriptural, God will receive into his family and own the little one committed to our keeping for a season. The rule is, "train up a child in the way he should go;" and the promise is, "when he is old he will not depart from it." This promise is fulfilled every day: because actual inquiry has demonstrated that by far the greater part of the ministers, elders, and private members of the Church, have sprung from a pious ancestry. It is no small distinction to have had a pious parentage. Well sang the poet:

"'Tis not my boast that I deduce my birth
From loins enthroned, or rulers of the earth;
But higher far my proud pretensions rise,—
The son of parents passed into the skies."

On the 2nd of March, 1819, in the town of Chillicothe, Ohio, an exceedingly feeble infant was born, giving but little promise of ever reaching mature life. At the proper time he was presented before the Lord and baptized ISAAC MELANCTHON COOK; where he was most solemnly dedicated to the Lord to serve Him in the Gospel Ministry, if his life should be spared. He was descended from the Scotch Irish, known the world over as the implacable foes of all civil or ecclesiastical tyranny, and at the same time as obedient subjects to all lawfully constituted authority; famed for their attachment to the Bible, the principles of Protestantism, and the doctrines and polity of Presbyterianism: who have impressed their character on a large portion of the American people, and at this time exercise a healthful and conservative influence throughout the entire nation. At the early age of five years he was deprived of both parents by death, and committed to the care of his maternal uncle, the late John Nevin, of Shippensburg, in this State. Here he was reared under the influence of household piety, the Bible, the shorter catechism, an orthodox ministry, and those works of solid worth which constituted the reading of intelligent Presbyterians of the past generation. And here no doubt were sown seeds that were buried for a long season, but at length produced a rich harvest. Principles were imperceptibly imbibed that were as lasting as life itself, and aided materially in developing and moulding the whole man. In youth he was characterized by an exuberance of animal spirits, a readiness to engage in all the sports and amusements of boyish pastime. And at the same time, he also manifested great quickness of temper, but was easily pacified and ever ready to acknowledge his error and to evince the reality of his repentance by lavishing kindness upon those whom he had injured or offended. Thus early did he exhibit a tenderness of disposition and a depth of feeling that shone all the more brightly when sanctified by grace. His body was never robust, and he was subject to severe attacks of sickness: though whatever he undertook was pursued with most determinate will, and as if possessed of a giant's strength. When about nineteen years of age, he went to Lacon, Ill. along with his sister and her husband. Previous to this he had manifested no special concern with regard to his own salvation. But in answer to the prayers of a few pious females, the Holy Spirit came down in that place; and he for whom special prayer had been made, was among the first arrested. Although it was not till after a long and painful struggle, under a deep conviction of sin, that he became a hopeful and joyous convert, his surrender to the Lord Jesus seems to have been more entire than is usual now among those who believe themselves Christians. It was not according to his nature—nor did he so understand the gospel—to attempt to serve God and mammon at the same time. All the ardor and impetuosity of his soul, excited and controlled by the highest of all motives—love to the Lord Jesus Christ—was brought into requisition. He looked upon himself as not "his own, but bought with a price." He interpreted and adopted in the true sense the teaching of the Apostle when he says: "None of us liveth to himself, and no man dieth to himself. For whether we live, we live unto the Lord; and whether we die, we die unto the Lord; whether we live therefore, or die, we are the Lord's." The claims of Christ superceded all others; the interests of the soul out-weighed all others. Thus an entire change took place in all the views and purposes of his life. His own determination is most probably expressed in advice given years afterwards to one who had just made a profession of religion—"Remember that it is very important that you should set out in your Christian life with a determination to make religion *the great thing.* Let it not *bend* to other interests, but make other interests *bend* to it. Aim at high attainments in the Christian life—and you will find your profit and your pleasure in it. The reason why so many have so little comfort in Christ is because they do not look for happiness to him—but to the world." The choice of a profession is of most momentous importance to every individual: it is not to be made lightly or without seeking divine direction, or from merely worldly motives—however common this may be. Isaac M. Cook wished to engage in that in which he might do most for the glory of God; and accordingly he anxiously and prayerfully turned his eyes towards the gospel ministry. But through the advice of his friends, on account of the feebleness of his bodily health and an impediment at times in his speech, he turned his attention to business; however, he was never satisfied with this arrangement. While engaged in selling goods, a voice within him not to be silenced seemed to be saying continually—" Wo is unto me, if I preach not the gospel." He heard the command of the master, " go work in my vineyard." He saw the fields white unto the harvest and that the laborers were few. He did not confer with flesh and blood: earthly pleasure and honor, and glittering wealth, had lost all their attractions. He pitied dying men, and the love of Christ constrained him. The 2nd of March, 1838, the anniversary of his birth, was a memorable day to him. Then he entered into solemn covenant with God to become a preacher of the everlasting gospel: this was not done without much self-examination and earnest prayer. Henceforth *for him to live was Christ.* But he did not rush into the battle without armor: he did not enter the harvest field before he was able to wield the sickle. He entered upon a regular and full course of preparatory study. Our Church has always been the strenuous advocate of an able and thoroughly educated ministry; her motto has ever been, " the priest's lips should keep knowledge." His academical studies were begun in the Academy kept at that time by Messrs. Nevin and Champ, in Sewickley, and completed at Jefferson College, Pa.—from whose halls so many able heralds of the cross have gone forth—where he graduated with credit in the autumn of 1841. During the progress of his studies he abounded in active labor for the salvation of souls, and was also assiduous in promoting the growth of piety in his own soul. Many now living can bear witness to the zeal and success with which he labored in the Sabbath schools, in the social meeting, and in private intercourse, to bring sinners to repentance. And if the hand of death had been then laid upon him, he would even at that time have accomplished more for the cause of Christ than most professing Christians do, who are allowed to fill up their three-score years and ten. After studying theology, partly at Princeton and partly under the direction of the Rev. Daniel E. Nevin, at that time pastor of the United Congregations of Fairmount and Sewickley, he was licensed to preach by the Presbytery of Carlisle.

We come now to the second part of his life—*his public ministry*. This was the great work of his life, and in this capacity he is principally known to the world and the Church. The "ministry of reconciliation," whether viewed in its origin, its objects, or results, is the highest and most responsible vocation to which man can be called; before it all other avocations sink into insignificance in divine estimation. It was instituted by God himself to make known his saving truth, to declare his mercy and love, and to exhibit the glory and power of heavenly grace. It has been appointed for planting and training the Church, for converting sinners, and for comforting and building up saints in their most holy faith. It is the first link in converting the sinner, and the principle means in "perfecting saints." It has been dignified by prophets and apostles, by Christ himself, and by good and holy men in every age. Those who bear this office are styled "ambassadors for Christ," and upon their work God has set peculiar honor. "How beautiful upon the mountains are the feet of him that bringeth good tidings, that publisheth peace; that bringeth good tidings of good, that publisheth salvation; that saith unto Zion, thy God reigneth." "But we have this treasure in earthen vessels, that the excellency of the power may be of God, and not of us." According to the appointment of God, the ministry is necessary to the very existence of the Church. Says Hooker—"Religion without the help of a spiritual ministry is unable to plant itself." The Church historian, Mosheim, observes, "that the best system of religion must either necessarily dwindle to nothing, or be egregiously corrupted, if it is not perpetually inculcated and explained by a regular and standing ministry." "Not even," says Calvin, "is the light and heat of the sun—not even is meat and drink so necessary for the support and cherishing of our present life, as the apostolical and pastoral office for the preservation of the Church on earth." The eminently pious Philip Henry, on the day of his ordination over a church only numbering at that time forty communicants, and which never during his whole labors there exceeded seventy, wrote "I did this day receive *as much honor and work* as ever I shall be able to know what to do with. Lord Jesus! proportion supplies accordingly." If Paul with all his natural gifts, his varied and large acquirements, and his miraculous endowments by the Holy Spirit, in view of the difficulties, greatness, and account to be given of the work, exclaimed, "who is sufficient for these things?" how should we shrink from the dread responsibility? But the same encouragement and strength is given us from on high, "My grace is sufficient for thee." It is not to be supposed that with his deep views of his own unworthiness and his high sense of the eternal responsibilities about to be assumed—with his warm feelings towards men and his burning zeal for God—and departed brother—could enter upon the sacred duties of the ministry, without being thoroughly penetrated by a sense of his own insufficiency and need of divine aid. Indeed, his dependence on the Holy Ghost, both with regard to himself and the success of his labors, was always conspicuous. After licensure, he preached occasionally in various places with much acceptance. For several months he labored in the congregation of Beaver and vicinity. When it became evident that it would be impossible to heal the divisions existing among the members of that congregation, a portion seceded, and formed the congregation of Bridgewater, selecting Mr. Cook for their pastor. The church at Bridgewater was organized by a committee of the Presbytery of Beaver, on the 29th of January, 1845, with 60 communicants; at the first communion 25 more were added by certificate. The field of labor to which he was now called was extensive and peculiarly difficult; requiring arduous and self-denying labors, great tact, and much of the spirit of Jesus. The dissensions in the old church had been violent and of long continuance, chief friends had been separated, the truly pious were discouraged, and not only Presbyterianism, but religion itself, had been brought into disrepute; and vigorous attempts at proselytism to another connection, never over-scrupulous in such things, had well nigh succeeded. The population was large, and the people upon whom he was to operate were widely scattered, and closely interlaced in many cases with other congregations. A new house of worship was to be erected, a new church was to be reared from the fragments of the old, and the people were to be moulded into the gospel pattern once more, and the whole community brought to feel the power of the truth. But through grace he was equal to the undertaking, and addressed himself to the work with characteristic energy. From the first he determined not to know anything among them, save Jesus Christ and him crucified. The great weapon he used was "the sword of the spirit," and most vigorously was it wielded in the sanctuary, in almost every school house within the bounds, and from house to house. By his kindness of manner, his evident devotion to his master, his determination of purpose, his faithful proclamations of the gospel, his searching appeals to the conscience—followed by the meltings of the Spirit—opposition disappeared like snow wreaths before the warmth of the sun. Christians received a new and gracious impulse, and grew in grace and attachment to him who was over them in the Lord: enemies became friends or held their peace from shame, sinners were awakened, "and much people was added unto the Lord." His ministry deserves to be ranked with the most successful of modern times, when all the circumstances are taken into consideration. At the organization of the church the communicants received were sixty-five, and at the first communion held shortly afterwards twenty-five more were received from the old church, so that the number with which he started was ninety communicants. At the time of his death the membership amounted to 325, while the congregation embraced 160 families. From the time at which the church was constituted until he *rested from his labors*—a period of nine years—142 were received into the church by certificate and 225 upon examination. According to this, allowing the whole time in which he labored in Beaver and vicinity, both before and after the organization of the Bridgewater church, to have been ten years, there was an average of over twenty-two added to the church every year by profession of faith! This was what would have been called a continuous revival, in many places. The most received in any one year were from March, 1845, to January, 1846, in which they reached the number of sixty-one; the greatest number received at any one time was in March, 1853, when thirty-one were received; the next largest accession was in March, 1852, when twenty-four were introduced to the visible Church. Nor were his labors confined to his own charge. He preached frequently in the neighboring congregations upon sacramental occasions and in seasons of revival, with marked effect. There are but few congregations in this region, and especially in the Presbytery of Beaver, where some fruits of his ministry cannot be found. He might decline to make visits when nothing higher than pleasurable enjoyment was intended, but when health and circumstances would at all permit, he never refused to preach "the glorious gospel of the Son of God." His labors were many and unremitting—often performed in the midst of much weakness and bodily suffering. He never expected long life for himself, therefore he redeemed the time allotted to him to the greatest advantage. Not only did he strive to convert sinners, but also to rear a vigorous and active church, and to train a consistent, praying, and laborious membership. The requirements of the Christian warfare were often and forcibly pressed upon their attention; and he urged them to come "to the help of the Lord—to the help of the Lord against the mighty." The various objects of Christian benevolence were regularly presented, and especially the claims of Foreign and Domestic Missions were urged with great fervor. The people were taught—and truly—that they had no more right to refuse to contribute of their substance for the relief of human misery and building up the Kingdom of God in the world, than to neglect prayer or any other religious duty. He took great interest in the Sabbath school and the religious training of the young. From desire to elevate the standard of education in the county where he dwelt, and extend its benefits, he consented to take charge of the Beaver Academy in December, 1852: and it was so conducted as to attain a degree of success never witnessed before, while his plans for future operations promised the most happy results. During the last years of his life he became anxious to be the means of introducing young men of talent, learning and piety to the gospel ministry, to which he attached increased importance, and looked forward to the time when it would be more esteemed by the world and better supported by the Church. So active was his life and so much was he abroad, that but little time was left for regular and systematic study, for everything else was made secondary to honoring God and saving men, though the most careful preparation was never considered unnecessary when possible. And lately when he was no longer required to devote so much time to purely missionary work, he began to provide materials for enlarged study and a more thorough culture. The greatness of pastoral work, the importance of correct Biblical exposition, the many forms of error that continually appeared, the many subtle enemies to be met, led him to value more highly than ever an able and learned ministry as well as one "wise to win souls." He was always an efficient member of Church Courts, and his correct business habits, and ready eloquence, afforded him great facilities for usefulness there. Some of his efforts in our Presbyteries, Synods and General Assemblies will long be remembered by those who witnessed and heard them. His circle of influence was rapidly extending in the community and in the Church. As might be expected, his own people were strongly and tenderly attached to him, and highly valued his efforts for their good. So necessary did he seem to their welfare, that notwithstanding his frequent attacks of severe illness, they did not think it possible he could be taken away. He had scarcely reached middle life: he had gone in and out before them so long: he had benefitted them so greatly: they loved him so much, and were so accustomed to meet him in the sanctuary, in the social meeting for prayer, at their fire-sides, and in the chamber of sickness, that they did not consider it possible to part with him. But God's thoughts are not as our thoughts, neither are his ways our ways.

The day of separation gradually approached. Disease, long lurking in his slender body, and feeding stealthily upon it, now assumed a fiercer character, and refused longer restraint. The skill of physicians was exerted in vain. The anxieties, prayers and tears of his people, who thronged his house and pressed to his bed-side, were unavailing. Nor could the long watchings, the tender soothings, the deep-drawn sighs, the almost breaking heart, and affectionate gaze of the partner of his life, detain him. Only he was calm and undisturbed. He knew on whom he had believed, and was persuaded that he was able to keep that which had been committed to him. That gospel he had so often preached, and which he so often commended to the sick and dying, was now his own support, consolation and joy. He gathered his Session around him, and gave them his parting counsel and blessing. He spoke of the preciousness of Christ, and his salvation, to all who came near, and sent for some to whom he had often spoken before of their immortal souls, entreating them once more to be reconciled to God. Dearly as he loved wife and children, and gladly as he would have lived to cherish her and rear them, and severe as were the pangs of nature in parting, yet he was enabled to commit them to a covenant-keeping God, with the hope that they would at length all be united again around the throne of God and the Lamb. The dark valley lost its gloom. The waves of Jordan had no terrors. Death was deprived of its sting, and the grave lost the victory. And when the shadows of the evening of the 10th of January, 1854, had gathered around his habitation, his disembodied spirit ascended where "there shall be no night: and they need no candle, neither light of the sun: for the Lord God giveth them light:" "and *there* shall be no more death." The people felt they had lost their best earthly friend, and that their church had been bereaved of a pastor whose place could scarcely be supplied. The whole community felt that their most public-spirited and enterprising citizen had been taken away. The churches round about felt that "a bright and shining light" had gone out. Ministers mourned the loss of one greatly blessed of God, "a brother beloved," and a most efficient co-worker, cut down in the morning—before it was noon—when apparently just maturing for the work to which God had called him. Two days afterwards, with heavy heart, we bore his body away from the place of his principal labors and triumphs, and placed it in the friendly soil of the beautiful valley of Sewickley, among the scenes and friends he loved so well.

Having given this rapid survey of *his youth* and *his ministry*, we are prepared to form some proper estimate of his character. In this there was much to admire, and many features that will be long remembered by those who knew him best. *As a man*, he was cheerful, kind and conciliating. His temperament was warm and enthusiastic—leading to energy and zeal in whatever he undertook. He was frank and open—free from deception—and affected nothing he did not feel. He was easy of access, and winning in his address to others. These qualities did much in attracting the people to him, and in preparing the way for him to approach them. He enjoyed the social circle, and sympathized deeply with the poor, the afflicted, and the disconsolate, while he could rejoice with the happy and prosperous. His friends he loved with passionate fondness. He admired the beautiful, the grand, and the sublime in nature, and could be charmed by poetry and thrilled by eloquence. Nor was he an inattentive observer of the course of the world, the changes of public opinion, and the indications of the future. *His relations as a husband and father were most happy.* But here is a sanctuary too sacred for us to enter. Here are scenes too pure for us to gaze upon. Here are memories too dear, tender and precious to be disturbed by us. They belong exclusively to those who enjoyed them, and who feel, but cannot express, the worth of these hallowed recollections.

> " To love, to bliss, their blended souls were given;
> In magic transport heart with heart entwined,
> And each, *though* happy, asked *a* brighter heaven."

As a Christian, his piety was sincere and genuine. At his conversion he had received a large measure of grace, and the cultivation of personal religion by reading the Bible, by self-examination, by prayer, by studying works of practical Christian experience, and by attendance upon the ordinances of the Lord's house, was his constant effort. Though comparatively weak in physical strength, and subject to frequent attacks of alarming sickness, there was nothing morose in his disposition: he was not subject to that sullen melancholy and nervous instability which so much interfere with the growth of piety, and hide the excellencies of practical religion from public observation. Physical condition has much to do with mental state, and physical condition, combined with mental state, has much to do in the beauteous and harmonious development of grace in the soul. Some seem cast in a coarser mould, so that the most delicate and finely wrought traits of Christian character never appear in them. In some, the light shines through a medium so defaced and discolored, that much of its surpassing beauty is never seen. But it was not thus with him; he was free and joyous in his nature, and equable in his temper, surrendering himself cheerfully to the transforming influence of heavenly grace; and his "profiting appeared to all." He knew the need that one who dealt with souls had of an experimental knowledge of the truths of the gospel, and that we are in danger of neglecting our own vineyard when attempting to keep that of others. Much time was given to secret prayer and private meditation; the tendencies of his own heart were closely watched, and every indication towards departure from God became a subject of earnest prayer and anxious endeavor: and he closely observed the effects of the truth upon himself. It was his desire to deal as faithfully with himself as with his people, and to bring every feeling, thought, and purpose into subjection to Christ. Bold and uncompromising before men when truth and right were at stake, yet he was always ready to uncover the head and bow the knee in the presence of "the King of Saints." *The most striking feature in his piety was his absorbing love for the Lord Jesus Christ.* This was his ruling passion; this lightened all his labors and sweetened all his toils; this is the key to his life and character. He cared for no question unless his Master cared for it; and the older he became, the more did he desire to do everything in the name of the Lord Jesus. He wished to preach to himself as well as to his people. On one occasion he writes: "Preached this morning at Bethlehem, from 1st Timothy, 1: 16, resulting in much comfort to my own mind, my heart being drawn out to admire and trust in 'God manifest in the flesh.' Oh, that my own heart might be more and more refreshed with the savor of the sweet truths that I preach." He frankly acknowledges one great hindrance to ministerial success to be in ourselves. Speaking of favorable indications among his people, he says: "A great trouble to me is my own heart; it is hard to keep; its want of liveliness is to me a grief and shame." In one place we find a record, describing, in a characteristic manner, his own deep sense of his own unworthiness, and the greatness of the love that redeemed him, and the grace that still supported him: "Sin—grace—one is mine, the other God's. Mine I see and feel would ruin me, if His did not prevent. How strange that any should talk of human goodness: I am a stranger to it. Once I *thought* I was a sinner—now I *know* it. How rich the grace that *can* save a wretch like me! Amázing—wonderful—glorious grace! 'In me there dwelleth no good thing.' Yet 'He loved me and gave himself *for* me.' O, the height and the depth of redeeming love! 'God forbid that I should glory save in the cross of our Lord Jesus Christ,' or preach aught else than 'Christ crucified.'

'Happy, if with my latest breath
I may but gasp his name,
Preach him to all—and cry in death,
Behold, behold the Lamb!'"

As a pastor, he was laborious, skillful, and successful. One of the most cheering promises of God to his people is, "I will give you pastors according to mine heart, who shall feed you with knowledge and understanding;" and one of our own poets has sung—

"'Tis not a cause of small import
The pastor's care demands,
But what might fill an angel's heart,
And filled a Saviour's hands."

He is the messenger of God—an under shepherd of the flock—a savor of life unto life, or of death unto death, in the message he delivers. He saves or condemns—prepares for glory in heaven, or for fiercer pangs and gloomier darkness in hell. The godly Scougal says: "So holy is our employment, that were our souls as pure as cherubs, as zealous and active as the blessed spirits that are above, we should yet have reason to cover our faces, and to be swallowed up in a deep sense of our own insufficiency for these things." The pastor deals with all classes and conditions—all grades of intellect and all degrees of morality, and encounters every variety of prejudice; and however different in other respects, they all are or have been ignorant and out of the way spiritually. Of some we must have compassion, making a difference; and others we must save with fear, pulling them out of the fire. Our departed brother was heavily burdened with the crushing responsibility laid upon him in his pastoral charge. Concerning two individuals almost Christians, he expresses himself: "I tremble at times lest they never become altogether such. Oh, for wisdom to bring sinners to Christ! What a meeting, O my soul, wilt thou have with this congregation at the judgment seat! Take heed, lest from the left hand some cry against thee." On the eve of a precious revival, he writes: "I rejoice with trembling; I cannot but hope the Master has come: I quake with fear lest we grieve Him away. Oh, for wisdom from on high to guide me aright—to keep me from doing aught amiss, or leaving needful things undone." He watched for souls as one that must give account, and was much in prayer for his people, and that the blood of souls might not be found on his skirts. He had—as every observant and conscientious Minister has, and as every Elder and private member of the church should have—a list of persons professedly destitute of grace, who were to be made the subjects of special prayer, and to save whom all lawful endeavors were to be used. He studied to interest his people in the subject of religion in every possible way: never was ambitious politician more anxious to secure votes than he to win souls. Much time was spent in family visitation, and in preaching the gospel from house to house, and in destitute places, where the word was often blessed to the con version of souls. He seized every opportunity of learning the religious state of those providentially thrown in his way. Impressed with the idea that his own life would be short, and of the greatness of his work, in the scriptural sense he became "all things to all men, that he might by all means save some." It was his custom to make much use of pungent tracts and books, such as "Baxter's Call," "Alleine's Alarm," and "Pike's Persuasives to Early Piety," which he would leave behind him, to deepen the impressions that had been made, and carry forward the train of thought that had been excited. And like Rutherford and M'Cheyne, whom he resembled in spirit, it was his habit to write letters and short notes, often accompanied with suitable tracts, to those under concern, or for whose souls he cared. Some of these were peculiarly happy in conception, and pointed in application. In one of these, directed to one who had not yet given her heart to the Lord, and from whom a sister had just been taken to heaven, he says: "Had death stilled your heart instead of *hers*, might not our lips have hesitated in saying, 'Our loss is her gain?' Would there not have been much room to doubt your happiness? Instead of being brightened with the light of heavenly hope, would not your grave have been overspread with gloom and filled with darkness?" And it was his constant effort to induce every Elder and every professing Christian to "endure hardness as good soldiers of Jesus Christ," as well as himself. He could not understand how any one could have any grace, and yet do nothing for the good of man or the glory of God. *But the public preaching of the Word was his chief confidence in the way of means.* In this he acted wisely. "For after that in the wisdom of God the world by wisdom knew not God, it pleased God by the foolishness of preaching to save them that believe." This is the great means appointed by God to convey the truth to the hearts and consciences of men: He has owned and blessed it in every age, and will never dispense with it. He has made it alike necessary to the conviction of the sinner and the sanctification of the believer. This was the work which our brother loved above all others. And for it he had some peculiar qualifications—a warm heart, a lively fancy, a glowing imagery, and an impassioned manner, together with a facility to make scriptural allusions, and use the figures of Scripture, which never fail to please and instruct. He never indulged in fanciful theories or dry and abstract argumentation; for them he had no liking. Every one before him was regarded as an immortal soul to be saved or lost, and consequently in imminent danger. The great doctrines of the Gospel were the themes he discussed. He could proclaim, in a startling manner, the terrors of the law, and describe with terrific vividness the horrors of hell. But he loved rather to speak of the mercy of God, the love of Jesus, the riches of saving grace, and the rest and glories of heaven. Like his divine Master, he loved to woo sin ners by compassion and tenderness; though, like Him, when the occasion demanded, his denunciations of the wrath of God against sinners were awful.

He was well acquainted with human nature—and knew the secret springs of action and how to "commend the truth to every man." It was his special delight to speak of Christ, his infinite condescension, his life, labors, sufferings, and death; of Christ in all his offices. And he had read, felt, thought, and spoken so much of his blessed Saviour, that his representations of him, like the ever varying hues of the kaleidoscope, though substantially the same—were ever changing—ever new—and always attractive. These are the truths best adapted to reach the heart and affect the conscience. By them did he most powerfully disturb the self-sufficient, awake the careless, alarm the wicked, and call upon the impenitent to repent and believe in the Lord Jesus Christ. The doctrines of the cross are those by which sinners must be converted and saints edified. In this way he always commanded attention, and never failed to make an impression for good; his words were often like nails fastened by the masters of assemblies. "Christ crucified—the great pervading theme of the gospel ministry, judiciously expanded, and closely applied—is itself a complete system of doctrines, a connected succession of duties, an unfailing supply of motives, an unexhausted treasury of hopes." So to speak of Christ and his salvation as always to attract the mind and affect the heart, is the real difficulty and the real triumph in preaching the gospel. *The pastorate was his delight, and he would not abandon it for anything else.* When urged by friends to resign his charge and intermit the active duties of the ministry for a season, on account of ill-health, he makes this significant remark—"I had rather wait for the Master in preaching the glad tidings." Success in his chosen work gladdened his heart and encouraged him to persevere. On Sabbath, the 20th of March, 1853, he makes this entry in his private journal: "Thirty-one received on examination—nine of whom I baptized; very encouraging and comforting is this day to me." But success did not lead him to forget his dependence on divine aid. Writing concerning the hereditary chief of the Chippewas, with whom he had conversed on the subject of religion, he said—"A more oppressively attentive auditor I have seldom had than he, as I tried to set Christ before him as a Saviour. I hope the Spirit dealt with him much more effectually than I." On a certain Sabbath he cries: "Saviour! Jesus! help me." Unworthiness and unfruitfulness is continually deplored. Near the close of the year he gives vent to his feelings—"Another year is almost gone! watching its ebbing life, two things astonish me: God's goodness and my ingratitude. May He forgive my follies past and mercifully grant me grace for days to come." When taking charge of the Beaver Academy he uses this language: "I must labor harder, for the night cometh wherein no work can be done." During the last year of his ministry he was more intensely desirous than ever to devote himself to the glory of God and the salvation of men. The fire within burned more intensely in proportion as the frail tabernacle in which it was pent up was consumed. The weaker the outward man became, the stronger grew the inward. On January 2nd, 1853, he expresses this hope, "This year may I increase in holiness, and more abound in works of piety and love." The intense energy put forth no doubt did much to suppurt and buoy him up, so that he lived longer than he would have done, had his days been spent "at ease in Zion." This record is made March 2d, 1853: "The anniversary of my birth! How swiftly the night passeth away: Saviour fit me for the day." He continued his beloved work of preaching the gospel until exhausted nature gave way. Even when the "silver cord" was breaking, he wrote "a word of exhortation and encouragement" to one who had lately put on Christ, and in whose case he had been greatly interested. To the last he was more anxious for souls than the most greedy miser for gold. A few days before his death he met with his Session, and that evening made this—his last entry in his private journal, too sacred for common gaze: "A sad thought that not even one should separate from the world." Soon that friendly death, so familiar to him, and of which he had so often thought and spoken, came to his relief: and "he being dead yet speaketh." What was said of another of kindred spirit may be said of him: "He has gone to the mountain of myrrh and the hill of frankincense, till the day break and the shadows flee away." His work was finished! His heavenly Father had not another plant for him to water, nor another vine for him to train; and the Saviour who so loved him was waiting to greet him with his own welcome—"Well done, good and faithful servant, enter thou into the joy of thy Lord." For "he was a good man, and full of the Holy Ghost and of faith: and much people was added unto the Lord."

By what has been said, we are taught what a vast amount of good may be accomplished in even a few years by one thoroughly imbued with the spirit of Jesus and intensely devoted to his service. It is not necessary for such an one to live long—his work may soon be done—and he may be early called to receive the crown. But *his works do follow him.* The slightest vibration of air is never altogether checked; the influence of a word once spoken never dies; an impression upon the heart in favor of the truth and holiness is never entirely removed. A "good work" once begun in the soul never ceases! What an influence, under God, for good has been sent forth in a short time by him of whom we have been speaking to-day, in all the congregations where he preached—in all the families he visited—in all the converts brought to the knowledge of the truth through him—in all with whom he conversed concerning eternal things—an influence ever widening and ever deepening as the endless ages of eternity roll on? How brightly will such servants of the Most High shine in the kingdom of heaven when compared with those who spend their days in grovelling among the things that perish, or with those who have solemnly dedicated themselves to the great work of saving souls, but who shrink back and turn aside fearing to "endure hardness as a good soldier of Jesus Christ?" We also learn that the *distinguishing* doctrines of grace so clearly revealed in Scripture and so distinctly stated by the Westminister divines—which were preached with such force and success by Paul and all the Apostles, by Athanasius, Luther,

Calvin, Whitefield, Livingston, Edwards, and the Tennents, have lost none of their power. However they may be misrepresented and maligned through ignorance or design, they are still "mighty through God to the pulling down of strongholds." They were preached in all their fullness by him whose departure we mourn, with undoubting mind, and they were *sharp arrows in the hearts of the King's enemies.*

Again, we learn the responsibility of those who enjoy a preached gospel. Christ said of those who did not receive the gospel—"If I had not come and spoken unto them, they had not had sin; but now they have no cloak for their sin." Christian brethren, it is a fearful thing to listen to the gospel from year to year, and yet not "grow in grace and increase in the knowledge of our Lord and Saviour Jesus Christ." My impenitent hearers, it is an awful thing to fall into hell from under the droppings of the sanctuary; the burnings of the unquenchable fire and the gnawings of the undying worm will be more terribly severe to you than to others.

Rev John D. Wells

Williamsburgh

Long Island

www.ingramcontent.com/pod-product-compliance
Lightning Source LLC
LaVergne TN
LVHW011139110826
845150LV00008B/2415

* 9 7 8 1 4 1 8 1 9 3 4 9 2 *